D1503428

Life is GOOD,
Life is HARD

Life is GOOD, Life is HARD

Meditations for Daily Living

JUDITH MATTISON

AUGSBURG Publishing House • Minneapolis

LIFE IS GOOD, LIFE IS HARD
Meditations for Daily Living

Copyright © 1987 Augsburg Publishing House

ISBN 0-8066-2272-5

All rights reserved. Except for brief quotations in critical articles or reviews, no part of this book may be reproduced in any manner without prior written permission from the publisher. Write to: Permissions, Augsburg Publishing House, 426 S. Fifth St., Box 1209, Minneapolis MN 55440.

Scripture quotations unless otherwise noted are from the Holy Bible: New International Version. Copyright 1978 by the New York International Bible Society. Used by permission of Zondervan Bible Publishers.

Photos: Dave Jorgenson, 12; Jim Whitmer, 30; Religious News Service Photo by John Greensmith, 58; Roger W. Neal, 80; Dave Anderson, 110.

Manufactured in the U.S.A.   APH 10-3838

1   2   3   4   5   6   7   8   9   0   1   2   3   4   5   6   7   8   9

This book is dedicated
to my sons
Ted and Michael,
who have given me more joy
than any words can express.
I love you!

CONTENTS

11 Introduction

Gratitude and Joy
14 A New Day
15 Spring
16 Greeting Card
17 Memories
18 Home
19 Senior Class Play
20 Alive
21 Retarded
22 New Year
23 Marriage Renewal
24 Reverence
25 Brothers
26 Toddler's Parade
27 Nap
28 Children
29 Individuality

Believing
32 Life's Design
33 Harmony
34 God's Grace
36 To Wonder Is a Beginning
37 Moments of Faith
38 Jesus' Suffering

39 Everlasting Arms
40 Meaningful Framework
41 Brain Tumor
42 Blessings
43 Believing
44 I Believe

Suffering
46 Despair
47 Life Isn't Fair
48 Communion Prayer
49 Our Presence
50 Irish Setter
51 Verification
52 Desolate
53 Sunday Morning Denial
54 Call to Resist Evil
56 Revelation
57 Abuse

Loss and Mourning
60 Reality
61 Self-Pity
62 Anticipation
63 Widow
64 Mourning Martin Luther King Jr.
65 Saying Good-bye
66 Separation
67 Moving On
68 No One Knows
69 Grieving
70 Life
71 Grandpa

72 Airplane Fears
74 Survivors
75 Preparation
76 Mourners
77 Too Late
78 Young Brother
79 Reunion

Struggles
82 Aging Parents
83 Depression
84 Responsible Son
86 Pleasure Pursuit
87 A Grandparent's Guilt
88 Bad Boy
89 Growing Up
90 One Person
91 Taking a Child to College
92 Feeling Insignificant
94 Tears
95 Bravery
96 Singular
97 Regret
98 Shielding Ourselves
99 Awkward
100 Capital Punishment
102 Prisons
103 Unemployed
104 Urbanization
105 Business As Usual
106 Vengeance
107 Belonging
108 Prophesy

Healing and Hope

112 Friendly Protection
113 Siblings
114 After Divorce
115 Comfort
116 Birthday Memorial
117 Strangers
118 Kenny
119 We Expect Too Much
120 Overload
122 Intimacy
123 Retreat
124 Battle
125 Change
126 Flash of Light
127 Promise

INTRODUCTION

It is human to hope that life will be a series of uninterrupted joys and satisfactions. We are disappointed when we encounter a setback in experiences of relationships, vocations, self-image, and health. Life is sometimes hard. It can be very unfair. It demands that we be persistent, hard-working, patient, and honest with ourselves. We live in an imperfect world and we are imperfect people. Life is hard.

Yet life is good! We have happy days and beautiful children. We experience the love and kindness of others and the richness of creation. We discover new learnings in the world and in ourselves. We have moments when we recognize that we have overcome adversity and we feel proud. Even our tears can refresh us as we release emotions and begin anew. Life is good.

This selection of thoughts and meditations are filled with life experiences. Some are painful and some pleasant, some full of joy and others a mystery. In all, they are a reflection of the journey we all travel, each with our different waystops, but all moving in our common humanity toward the living God. Although we may rage at God for our unhappy and confusing times, we also praise God that we are always forgiven and cared for; that life can be fun and rewarding. Whatever life holds, we know that even our human vulnerability and inadequacy is good because it makes us open to the loving protection and guidance of God, in whatever form God is revealed to us. Life is good. Life is hard. In these pages I proclaim, with the writer of Deuteronomy,

"Choose Life!"

GRATITUDE AND JOY

"Sing to the Lord with thanksgiving."
(Psalm 147:7)

A New Day

I woke up this morning!
Praise God—
one never knows, after all.
There was sunlight
and a stretching breath.
God lives
and I, too.
I shall go out
to meet God again
and again
this day.
Perhaps today
God is among the poor
or in the roots of trees
growing nearby.
Surely
God is in the sun
and Son
and life.
I rejoice!

Spring

I want to live to know a hundred springs!
To feel aroused,
to run across the sun,
and to close my eyes to hear new birds more dearly—
to watch the rain transform the grass
from tired to green,
and to cherish moments fancying the day
when I will reunite seedlings with their earth
or find the irises ready to reveal
their graceful blooms to all the world.
These are the times when I pull
the muddy, sweet smell of earth into my lungs
and send its welcome excitement to every fingertip.
I want to live to know a hundred springs!

Greeting Card

*I*n the white envelope,
inconspicuously familiar,
was sealed our loving friendship:
the laughing and
bickering and the
alternate lifting of one another
upon powerful shoulders
so that the languid one
could see the magnificence
of life's parade.
Our sharing,
our caring,
our hope for an enduring bond
through our expectant tomorrows
was in their promise—
script more poetic than windsong.
    "We love you both very much."
Thank God for friends,
for love.

Memories

When I look back
      in search of significant memories
it will be the lives
I have touched
which will carry me across the years.
The hands that took my pussywillows
and exclaimed thank you,
the ones who saw my tears
and did not run away,
the momentary glimpses of love
which took my face into gentle hands
and made me smile,
the human tenderness
which made me search
for the will to go on—
even into the unexpected—
believing and hoping.

Home

*I*n this place
    I am.
I need not pretend.
nor bear the load of crowds.
Here I can be alone
or laugh with friends,
share my tears,
my gentle self,
and listen to my children.
Love lives in this place—
home.

Senior Class Play

*I*t took six weeks of rehearsing
every night after school—
good weeks,
hard working and laughing,
frustration.
Mom became impatient—
I was late for dinner again.
I pleaded our necessity,
our goal.
She was annoyed, but still.

We did well.
They laughed and applauded
(even our peers)
and we felt proud.
We bowed,
and someone brought me roses—
a dozen!
I was thrilled!
Now, remembering, I am touched.
Tucked inside, a card—
"Love, mom."

Alive

*T*here is part of me—
    spirit
    unseen
    unspeakable—
which renders words inadequate
and cannot be described.
A consuming moment,
a sense of otherness
which may come in awe
at a quiet night breath,
a child's birth,
or in mystery and fear
when death's terror overcomes me
and I refuse to succumb
yet cannot escape finitude,
or in an absolute conviction
of knowing right.
This essence of my being,
glimpsed only briefly
but undeniably powerful,
is that part of me
called "God's image."
In those moments
when I am most certainly
Creature
I am, finally, Truthful,
and made in the image
of God.

Retarded

*H*er retarded mind is
compensated by a
joyful soul.
A child
forever.
A willing spirit,
yielded to love even in
the midst of anger.
God has blessed her
clouded mind
with a sunshine view.

New Year

*I*t is a significant thing
   to mark another year's passing.
I write it out—
   what I have learned this year
   what has been good
   who I have loved
   and that which I would choose to forget.
The lesson is that life goes on.
I am forgiven
   and I need not punish myself.
   Rather, like David
   I begin again.
Life goes on
   steals away
   and if I would only pause,
   create more moments for myself
   when I think about life's meaning,
   I would value life more.
I pause—set myself apart, alone.
   I ask myself
      who would I choose to be?
   Do I feel the full impact of living?
      All the feelings—
      sadness, happiness, anger, and fear?
      Is every moment dear?
I would take time to realize
that every day is a new year's day,
and love the gift of life.
Begin again.

Newness

Ps.   33: 1-5

Judith Matthison -
    New Year
        Individuality

Gracious God –

We praise you
for beginnings-- for
~~the~~ newness of life,--
for the refreshing times
together. We give thanks
for the ~~times~~ together
tonight and for all
of your ~~servants~~ people here
who gather in your name
with the desire to serve
you better. We especially
give thanks for those
who have accepted the
challenge to be our
leaders. Give them
your grace so that they
may have the strength
& courage to lead us
as women ~~of the ELCA~~
here @ NHLC.

Marriage Renewal

*I*t takes time.
Time to gather all the crumbs,
anecdotes,
and small events;
to sort them out, laugh, decide, and
brush them aside.
Only then do we begin
to share the loaf,
our feelings;
who we are today—
who we have become through the hours
when we ran past each other,
   harried breakfasts
   separate schedules
   dinners of chatter
   and gone again—
until we sat
in the white light of television
silent, tired.
Sometimes we forget the possibility
of pleasure and surprise
that comes from honestly sharing,
being close
with those we love
and discovering we have grown.
But it takes time
alone, together.

Reverence

One cold November morning
I took grandma to the polls to vote.
It was windy
and, for grandma, difficult to walk.
As we left, she pointed
to the dark brick schoolhouse walls
where sparrows clung,
hovering and chirping in the cold.
"Look at the little birds,"
she clucked in her Norwegian brogue.
"Their feets is so cold!"
Despite her encumbrance
she had felt compassion
for the struggle of small creatures.
Such reverence for living things!

Brothers

*H*appy in the sun,
     two small boys
walk to the neighboring green,
one leading,
the other following in run-steps,
talking.
They stoop to see a frog
run,
then wait for one another.
If we could only
keep the moment,
we would be kept
forever young.

Toddler's Parade

A hooded sweatshirt
    underneath
a red umbrella
struts
across our lawn
saying, "march, march"—
patriot of a land called
Childhood.

Nap

*B*less the small boy
asleep in the front hall at twilight,
in his crumpled jacket, with a
lunchbox snack beside him—
too tired to go another step,
play another game,
find another acorn,
or watch another bird.
This little person
brought me dried weed flowers
and told me "I love you."

Children

*T*hey walk the sidewalk
     or drive in heavy-duty plastic cars.
Small beings
   full of as much mystery
   and potential for life
   as the tulip sprouts of spring.
They remain our hope—
   the ones who ask questions
   and lie on grass, humming,
   watching clouds.
They know what we avoid—
life is not clocks or roads.
It isn't even being right.
Life
   is letting in the sunrise
      because it's new
   and getting ice cream on fingers
      and collars
      because it tastes good.
Life is laughing without thought
and crying when we cannot
   find an answer
   or a reason
   or a friend.
Life is now
   and love is fresh—
   in God.
The children know.

Individuality

*E*very person,
a gift.
Packaged in
various papers
one chooses to wear.
Bound by one's own
self-image,
and crowned with
a delicate bow
of love.

Take care
when you open
each package.
Each is fragile.
The one who lies within
has immense possibilities.
Gently,
tenderly,
lovingly open each gift.
And behold
the work of God
shared with you.

BELIEVING (FAITH)

"Immediately the boy's father exclaimed,
'I believe; help me overcome my unbelief!' "
(Mark 9:24)

Life's Design

*L*ife
isn't a carefully cut
jigsaw puzzle
of events and people
waiting to be placed together
in a comprehensible design.
Life is pieced together
from the fragile fragments
of broken dreams,
an abandoned gas station
on a lonely country road,
and mysterious anticipation
of waiting for a baby to be born.

Harmony

*G*od calls.
  Each one hears
a different wavelength of the sound.
For each one
has an ear, distinct,
and experiences
unlike any other.
Listen, people.
Hear
the vast magnitude
of sounds
which God emits.
Then, sing!

God's Grace

*B*ecause her father drank
and life was unpredictable
she learned to watch others
very carefully,
measuring their pauses
and studying their eyes.
And because when he was sober
he sometimes hit her,
   burned her small hand,
or thrust cruel weapons into her—
   a twisted coat hanger
   a hot curling iron
   a hairbrush
   himself—
she identified with those oppressed
and felt the pain of suffering ones
and cared.
She learned to value children
and protect them,
and to value life
because it might so quickly
be stolen away.
At thirteen she promised herself
she would not go insane.
She saved her memories
and her observations of the others
   their pain
   their love
   their eyes
and turned them all to poetry.

It was God who spared her—
    gave her the will to survive,
    love from strangers,
    an unexpected, unexplained
    sense of the goodness of life,
and the belief that people
could be trusted.
Now she lives!
Joyous
because she knows
    her body is strong
    her spirit is full of life
and her God
never abandoned her.

To Wonder Is a Beginning

I have wrestled
with so many questions,
noticed inconsistencies,
doubted miracles,
and looked for proofs.
I get tired of trying to believe.
There are others
who seem to have their faith
in place—
    sure,
    steady,
    unperturbed.
Yet from childhood
I've wondered
and searched,
sighing as I traveled on,
relentless in my need
to know.
Occasionally I realize,
to wonder is a beginning
and to question presumes an answer.
I realize I believe,
in spite of myself.

Moments of Faith

I am still a bit too proud
to admit how much I need
to give in.
Occasionally I catch a glimpse
of a faith that says
"I am not to be explained—
that is what faith is;
trust."
I see it for a moment,
then I fearfully compute my system;
I program believing
into thought or theory
or familiar phrases
which I have read
but someone else has lived.
Yet those short surges of belief
carry me on, hopeful.
If air breathes fresh
and unrestrained,
if love surrounds me
beautifully strong enough to
make me trust,
if I can feel God
for even just a moment
I may yet live.

Jesus' Suffering

I get some sort of
morbid satisfaction
reliving your pain
your death
each Lent.
Your suffering touches me.
I understand
your sadness and
I try to understand
your mission.
Let me not glean only
surface meanings—
feeling sorry for you,
shocked or
temporarily repentant,
meditative.
You are living now.
And you look to see if I
will also move beyond the pain
to active change,
Alive!

Everlasting Arms

*I*t sounds strange
but I wish I could be rocked
in a rocking chair
like my mother did so long ago.
I need comfort,
someone to hold me
and tell me it's all right.
I need to pull away from the world
and go within myself
where a lullaby can assure me
that there is rest
and hope
and God.
The melody comes to memory—
   Children of the heavenly Father
   safely in his bosom gather
   nestling bird
   nor star in heaven
   such a refuge e'er was given
Rock, rock,
in the everlasting arms of God.

Meaningful Framework

Without God
      there is no humaneness,
no contrast,
no goal,
no purpose to be.
Only minutes marked on a clock
that runs until it is emptied
and life ends.
All else is but animal—
living, scratching, being,
dying.
Without God
there is no framework
on which to position existence,
no light
against which I can see
eternity
or me.

Brain Tumor

*T*error.
  The doctor reports a brain tumor
in the young mother.
All the family fights desperately
to believe it can be all right,
that she can live
and be whole again.
Tears, panic,
deep concern for the two little boys
who may be motherless
after surgery.
Then, unexplained
calm.
Quiet.
Acceptance of the moment,
will to face the unknown,
joy in the gifts of love.
Waiting in peace,
held in the hand of God.

Blessings

I read about the concentration camp
and wept,
"Dear God, it is not gratitude
to count my blessings,
feeling proud of the list
and overfed today.
Nay! thanks-giving
comes from awareness
of the existence of evil,
the presence of death,
the weakness of humans
(including me),
and the redeeming chance to share,
because I'm given one more hour
to live!
Thank God!"

Believing

*R*ight, wrong, black, white
ought, should.
These measures bleed
like a watercolor on a
tissue life-fabric.
Who can say the truth?
Perhaps the only truth
is that we may never know
all truths,
but that we've lived out
what we believed.
We've dared to hope and
we've risked the pain
of knowing or
of disappointment.
The painting is in the stroke
of caring enough to go on
believing.

I Believe

*T*oday I believe in people.
 I believe in a doctor who cries
and in friends who wait—
that people sing to themselves
even when they are alone.

I believe that black nights
calm a tired traveler
and embrace lovers;
that a small boy
can belong to all mothers
and love any homeless dog.

I believe that sunlight
dances on the floor of anguish
and warms the toes of those
who long for the touch of smiles.
I believe in people
   in good.
I believe in life.

SUFFERING

"Come to me, all you who are weary and burdened,
and I will give you rest."
(Matt. 11:28)

Despair

*I*n the course of one morning
two men stood by my office door,
one speaking slowly and quietly,
the other tense and agitated—
both of them afraid to live.
"I could hardly get up this morning."
"I sat and did nothing all day."
Their tears sat poised,
unable to flow,
or held back for fear they might not cease.
My arms wanted to hold these men
whose spirits were barely surviving
for reasons too complex to discern.
They needed the food of love
and someone to listen,
the courage to be angry,
or cry
and a reason to go on.
I knew I could not give another person
the reason—
it must be set free from within.

Life Isn't Fair

S he was snatched away
without warning or illness—
twenty-seven,
beautiful and vibrant with life.
The graveside mourners
could not bear to leave.
Her husband, speechless,
her family distraught
and all around them
silence and tears.
Silence.
It is not fair!
And there are no answers to
why?
It is God's will we should live
and be happy
and take care of each other.
Yet, again and again we discover
we are only humans;
people are hurt
and they die—
even at twenty-seven.
Life is not fair.
Our only comfort—
God weeps with us and welcomes her Home.
Take care of each other.
Life isn't fair.

Communion Prayer

*A*s she leaned upon the rail
I prayed,
for she cried so—
weary and deeply penitent.
Her face was living anguish.
She came to be forgiven,
but she walked away
heavy with a guilt
she could not yet resign.
Oh dear woman,
it will surely pass!

Our Presence

We stumble on those
who hurt so deeply
they cannot trust,
and dare not believe
for fear of betrayal
or loss.
We problem-solve or listen
or pray the pain will go away.
Day after day
we wait to see
what may never be—
wholeness.
Yet we must wait
and stand beside
for it is the steady hand,
the repeated kindness,
the patient ear,
which may bring hope.
Those who suffer
do not need our answers.
They need our constancy,
even when we're tired
or rejected or confused.
We who believe in an
Everlasting Presence
give the best help by saying,
"Whatever happens,
I'll be there."

Irish Setter

*T*he young Irish setter broke from its master's lead
into city traffic, and lay dying.
The man carried his bleeding body to the sidewalk
and after putting it down
violently cast the leash to the ground.
Cars paused, and we called out an offer to help.
Go away! he yelled. Go away!
and flung his arms to drive us from him.
He paced, and bowed his body at the waist.
He squeezed his palms about his head.
He was unable to cry.

When human beings decided
that crying was beneath them,
they took on untold suffering,
self-contained anguish, anger, pain.
We reject our human need to express ourselves,
pretend to be stronger than human,
try to be God.
God must surely cry for us as we suffer so.
We are too proud.
Even Jesus wept.

Verification

I climbed the stairs to church
in reluctant haste
hoping to discover it was not true.
Just a bad rumor
a disturbing dream
but surely not true.
Where else could I know
but in church?
The woman announced
our community sorrow—
their son had died
(of a shot to his own head).
My mind heard his mother scream
and saw his father
collapsed in tears—
my friends!
My body trembled.
His own son not spared.
Her child dead upon the world's cross.
It is true.

Desolate

*H*er voice on the phone
surprised me,
late at night and desperate.
"I'm alcoholic!
I'm at the treatment center.
I feel so desolate.
When I get out I need someone.
Will you be there?
Maybe just to go to a hockey game.
I feel so desolate.
Will you be there?"

I hesitated.
I didn't want to be there.
I was afraid to commit myself
to one I hardly knew—
even one who needed me so much.
She must have heard rejection
in my halting reply, "Yes."
She never called again.
I've never known what happened.

Sunday Morning Denial

*S*he weeps in church,
 tears barely perceptible
as she bites the inside of her
drooping, despondent cheeks.
She came alone.
Her husband couldn't rouse himself
after the night before.
"He still gets to work every day,"
she consoles herself.
It's the Saturdays—and Friday nights
and the silent, heavy Sundays
when he will not talk
except to reprimand
her worried leading questions.
She knows that something's wrong—
somehow life and liquor
have become unbalanced.
But they cannot talk
except in sarcasm or pleas or shouts.
She can only come to church
and cry,
and hope that he will want to change
before she starts to hate.
She wants to help,
but she has searched for no one
who can show her
what to do.
To search would be to say
she knows
she must begin.

Call to Resist Evil

I have met evil in person.
  Raw power—
      violation
      pain
      screaming—
and the systematic withdrawal
of nurturing
so that the damage
lies beneath the bruises
as well as in the wounds.

I have held the victim
limp in my arms
unable to resist anymore
and afraid to be open
to the nurturing
which could heal the wounds
and ease the pain.

Rage!
Rage against the evil!
Fight it in all forms—
most especially evil which is
seductive
and insidiously oppressive
so that one chooses not to fight
from lack of self-respect
or fear of failure.

Rage—
fight the cancer
which destroys from within.
Flail, scream, fight!
Give power to the life
which is intended to survive!
Rage against the evil!

Revelation

I talked to a man
who lives in hell
every day.
"People will let you down.
Sooner or later,
they all dump on you," he said.

"Where's the gospel?" I pleaded.
"The reality of God
present in human beings?
It is in human relationships
that we meet God!"

"I know God," he said.
"But I know people.
It's human nature—
people hurt you."

Sad, I left him with a hug,
wishing he could accept kindness,
believe in caring,
in Christian love.
Sad, I reaffirmed my gratitude
for persons who have loved me.
Those who, with their caring,
have overcome the human nature
which would have destroyed me.

The man lives in hell,
because he can't believe,
trust,
that there is Good.

Abuse

*T*he tragedy of child abuse
is that the child believes
that pain and torture
are deserved.
A child thinks
if people treat me badly,
I must be bad.
If they don't love,
I'm unloveable.
If I'm abused,
it is a way of life—
for a child has no other guides
than the elders' actions
and the limited experiences
of its world,
its feelings.
For the child there is no wrong
or right,
only today,
and what happens.
It takes a lifetime to unlearn
that one is not worthwhile;
but deserving of love and care.
Only if God is there
in someone else who stays
and loves
and believes in the child
will the person learn to trust.

LOSS AND MOURNING

"[Jesus] fell with his face to the ground and prayed,
'My Father, if it is possible,
may this cup be taken from me.' "
(Matt. 26:39)

Reality

I was eighteen.
Mother called me to her room
to say the truth, the pain.
"I know I will die.
I know God wants me."
Tears of despair and love
overwhelmed me as I begged
that it not be true,
but I knew—
she was too tired now.
Life had taken away her spirit
and drained her body.
Somehow I would have to live
with the reality of death
and the pain of separation—
the sense of abandonment
when a mother leaves a child behind.
I would have to wait
for God to help me understand.
I sighed, and wept,
and walked away,
changed forever.

Self-Pity

*H*er husband died.
And she with him,
retreating from the world
and hiding from her son
by sleeping away her days
solitary
in her room.
She felt she had no reason
to go on.
Then one day her son
stood in the doorway,
weeping.
"Sometimes I miss dad so!"
Her mind and heart shook,
aware of her self-pity
and his honest need.
She rose,
ministered to him,
and began to live again.

Anticipation

*H*er mother is failing
and it's only a matter of time
the doctors say
until she will be gone.
She spends a lot of time
visiting her mother
and welcoming her for dinner.
She cherishes the days
the hours.
Yet they are also painful.
"It's hard when you know
that every time you see her
it's one time less. . . ."

Widow

Nobody thinks
  she cares anymore,
seventy-two and alone now.
Her husband gone,
she's one among couples.
But when the music plays,
romantic and gentle
in the evening,
she misses him
and remembers—
it was good then.
Nobody realizes
she still needs him;
his affection,
his warmth,
his kindness,
his love.

Mourning Martin Luther King Jr.

*S*omehow I am glad
to be a part
of this great sorrow.
For, within the depth
of tears and
soul-filled singing,
lies a vision.
As I'm sharing
in the anguish,
finding solace in the
Lord,
I have found a hope,
a reason and
a dream for which to live.

Saying Good-bye

*F*acing one another
   I could see her eyes glaze
as she prepared to leave her home,
facing change reluctantly.
I encouraged her,
"You have a good husband
and a new life.
Trust that it will all go well."
She looked at me
and said, "It's you. . . ."
I knew at once!
It isn't change—
it's loss
which brings her tears.
Not years ahead
but years behind
and memories and hugs
and love.
I could not see
as tears welled up in me.

Separation

I wait so long to have it over with
and then, it's over with
and I cannot bring him back

and the sobs which fill the room
    the cries
    the pain
empty my body
    from the very back of my being
rise above the mountains
into the distance
longing to pull him back
to see the smile
to reach for the comfort
to plead
    don't go
only to know he cannot stay
even when his tears say he wants to.
This is the pain
of love and separation

that Jesus knew
    pleading to stay
    having to go
knowing the Father of Mountains
watches it all with us
and holds us,
crying with us
because it must be so
if we would call it love at all.

Stay.

Moving On

I'm sick of moving on,
leaving the love behind,
starting over,
building new relationships,
wondering whether tomorrow
offers spring
or warm firelight.
Don't tempt yourself
with tomorrows—
they only compromise todays
and spoil the joy of now.
Don't depend on someone else.
Your joy resides within you
and tomorrow never comes.
Still. . .
it's painful here alone.

No One Knows

*T*he saddest part
about having you gone
is that no one
seems to understand
the depth of my loss.
I don't expect them
to make the pain subside.
There are no magic words
to replace your presence
in my emotional balance,
my heart.
But I struggle so
feeling desolate,
because no one seems
to understand
how much I cared,
how much I lost.

Grieving

*G*rief comes unexpectedly,
driving down the street
tears blur my vision.
A song evokes a memory
and I reach to the empty space
where your warmth
used to wait for me.
In the middle of a busy day
I feel suddenly alone.
Surely God understands
and weeps with me
comforting me
until this loss subsides,
sobs to tears to sighs
and silence.
Begin again.

Life

*T*o live
    is comprehending death;
to see the majesty of snow
is to know
that it will disappear,
and love it.

Grandpa

Grandpa wasn't afraid to die.
I asked him
as he lay in the hospital bed.
He only hated to leave his darling behind.
He understood better than I
how lonely grandma would be.
"I won't go home again," he said
and tears which I had saved
through several years of dread
dripped from my cheeks to the floor.
"Better in this bed than gone," I sighed.
"I'll miss you."
He clutched my hand to comfort me
and to say his thanks for my love.

We reminisced and he too cried for
"Mumsy," his wife,
and my mother,
    the daughter so dear to him in life
    he could never give her away in death
    though she had left us both
    long before he stood ready to depart.
In a mixture of loving sadness,
and a mysterious joy of having shared
the fullness of the moment,
unafraid to say it all,
I left his room
and he soon left my sphere of the living.
But still in the texture of the skin of my hand
is his warm grasp,
our tears and our love.

Airplane Fears

*M*other died when I was green
and young, confused
and feeling so in need of her.
It took some time
before I knew I hated that she left
even though I knew she couldn't help it.
Mother was gone
and the vacant moments
never really go away.
Today I leave on business
to fly from my small sons—
unwilling to cause them my former pain
and loneliness.
I cannot stay because I know
to stop my life and growing
because I've known sadness in the past
is not to live
but to die with mother
over and over.
Still, when I think of leaving them
I am overwhelmed with tears
at all I want to say, to show,
and all the love I still possess
and wish to give my boys.
I am afraid to go,
afraid that I might not return
to love them.
Afraid they will not understand.
I can only hope my fears
are temporary confrontations

with the finite gift of living,
and that I will soon return
and hold my boys
and life
more dear.

Survivors

*S*he was very ill
for years
and let herself die
without telling anyone.
Those who loved her
were stunned
when doctors offered no hope
for one so young as forty.
In two weeks she was dead
and they were left
in shocked misery,
wondering.
How could no one know?
Why would she choose to go?
After the initial grief
little by little
thoughts crept in.
Was there something they had done
or not done
which led her to despair?
Where was God
when she was weakening
and scared?
What of her children
and her parents, overcome?
Where was God!
Was there nothing they could have done?

Preparation

We look on at death
    curiously
amazed at the size of the funeral crowd
sensationalizing unusual tragedies
retelling the pain of others.
We do not mean to be unkind,
but we are insulated
day to day
from the totality of life—
and death catches us unaware,
unsuspecting.
We would prepare
by watching carefully
to see how others react,
observing what separation does to the living.
Our sympathy is framed
with curious calculation
because we are not able
to absorb in our souls
what changes death will bring to us
and we are afraid to know.

Mourners

*D*eath.
    Sorrow's vacuum
draws in friends who care,
who can fill the void
and share the burden.
They are pulled in a rush
of sympathy and compassion
at the first shock of separation.
The intensity diminishes
as feet tread home
weary
drained.
The supporters float gently away,
released from anguish.
The sorrow remains for
those most deeply hurt,
now left trapped in the emptiness—
the vacuum of absence.

Too Late

I had so hoped
that she would read my book.
It was only a month more
but she could not wait.
Parallel lines,
earnest, but never joining.
How selfish of me
to want to extend her life
for my own pleasure—
but how human.
Always promises, unkept,
always plans, unlived;
toys left in the yard are
blanketed by winter snow.
Death steals the tomorrows
and todays,
and leaves us with only
the quiet breezes of yesterdays.

Young Brother

*T*he little boy was frightened
"It's all right, mom,
it's all right,"
was all that he could say.
His mother was crying
and he did not know
how he could calm her.
Or restore her strength.
He needed her to lean on.
It would be several hours,
even days or years,
before he would understand
how pained and weak
a mother feels
when her child has died.

Reunion

*H*e had grown accustomed to her absence,
   painful though it was,
for she had been gone now for years,
and one learns to substitute other joys—
   new friends
   different patterns
   other homes.
When the invitation came
to return to the church anniversary
he was happy to renew relationships
which had been part of their early years.
He embraced friends
and laughed
and together they shared stories,
   pictures
   memories. . . .
Then suddenly he felt the empty spot,
the reality.
She was not there.
He began to cry.

STRUGGLES

"My grace is sufficient for you,
for my power is made perfect in weakness."
(2 Cor. 12:9)

Aging Parents

*I*t's not so much that we expected
them to live forever.
It's just that we thought
or hoped
they wouldn't have to change.
Somehow they would remain
as powerful, alert
and self-sufficient
as they had always seemed to us
who watched them from behind,
in awe.

The flower of the dandelion
not only fades
but crumbles into fragments
before it blows away.
We had hoped to hold on
to the golden dandelion
until the very last,
and set it free.
But the life design is not so.
We have not such power.
It is the day-to-day loss,
the crumbling of a fragile soul
that we mourn.

Depression

Waking to a world
      of clouds and low air,
I trudged into morning.
Having once decided
to be lonely,
I was.
Gray sky eyes,
disposition dreary,
weary,
uninspired to see
ahead;
a profitless decision.

Responsible Son

A child,
he tried his best
to please his parents
   practiced piano
   kept his shoes shined
   got good grades
   and tried to act grown-up.
His eyes looked up eagerly
for their approval
but dropped with a sigh
when it never came.

Now forty,
he has succeeded in his work,
though his parents seldom notice.
He tries to please others
   his boss
   his colleagues
   his own high expectations.
It is as if his parents
stand looking over his shoulder
   comparing
   remembering mistakes
   expecting agreement
   and rigid.
His chest heaves in disappointment.
His mind and heart tell him
"Harder, harder—
you must try harder."

They will never be satisfied
and his disappointment is not
that he isn't good enough
for his family to love—
but that they are not
capable of loving him
and he wonders if he's ever had
any family at all.

Pleasure Pursuit

We look for "highs"
    momentary pleasures, so exciting
that they take our breath away
or leave us smiling in the morning.
We move from one to another
always new—
from sports cars
to hot tubs,
art forms and culture
on to the sport of people,
    meeting the exotic,
    the strange,
    and the mysterious
in a game of life
where relationships are pretending,
in the search for someone new
and another high.
It is a dismal failure.
We avoid commitment to cause
or to love when it requires sacrifice.
We never feel humanity
    only observe it
and keep our tears on swizzle sticks
where they cannot cleanse our souls
nor change our hearts and direction.
A masquerade of life,
we never know the depth of Jesus
because we dare not risk reality
and die without our "high."

A Grandparent's Guilt

*T*he grandmother's eyes
      clouded with tears
for grandchildren—
unsuspecting—
whose parents parted,
unable to maintain marriage
amidst the wrenching
of our dynamic lives.
"I feel guilty," she said,
"that my children have not
made good marriages."
There was no answer
and her only relief
was her tears.

Bad Boy

All the children knew
he was a problem to everyone.
I cannot recall his name—
I'm sorry, because a name
seems sometimes the only thing
which is truly ours.
He lived in those small houses
back away from the country road
where I could never go.

He did strange things
and teachers called him naughty.
Once he did something
we weren't supposed to talk about
but we did.
"Bad boy," ten years old.

He drowned in a creek
that passed near his home.
Those days I guess we thought
it was his due, to die—
he wouldn't be a problem anymore.
Now I wonder.

Growing Up

My little son
ran to the neighbors' today
all by himself
for the first time
to play.
He talked all the way!
He was excited!
I smiled at his eager
independence.
And then—
suddenly I cried.

One Person

*N*o one in the family was sane,
not one.
Each saw life and people
in distortion,
save one.
The middle son,
surrounded by delusion
and confusion,
somehow learned that he
was loved
and how to interact
with others.
The doctors were perplexed.
How?
Who kept his mind and life
bearable, consistent?
One woman.
She gave him milk and cookies
many days when he stopped by
as he walked from school to home.
One consistent, loving person.
One!

Taking a Child to College

*T*he child in arms
   grown tall and lean
is ready to begin to live adult.
We are pulled taut
between holding on
and letting go—
the joy of vicarious achievement
and the pain of realizing
that life is short
and nothing ever stays the same.
The promise of their future
gleams in our tears of loss.
Only God stays the same.
Human beings weep to say
good-bye.

Feeling Insignificant

*I*t's been a rude awakening.
  Gradually I've grown
aware of how brief life is—
    my aging,
    my insignificance in an over-
    populated world.
I've always known it
    but lately I feel it.

Sometimes I'm jolted
to think that all my efforts,
maybe my whole life,
will not make an impact.
I get a queasy feeling when
I think of that phrase
"A hundred years from now,
who'll know the difference?"
Who will?

I think I need help, direction.
Maybe the only way to find meaning
is to be involved with other people.
Other people may not make me
immortal,
but they will help me feel alive.
You taught us, Lord,
that love is never wasted,
never defeated.
It never dies.

Perhaps the message
of the church
and Scriptures is that
life itself is the human struggle
of wanting immortality
but learning to live
with the truth.
The Truth is that
life has meaning
only if we experience it;
fear, delight, frustration.
And sometimes feeling insignificant
is part of our appreciation of living experience.

Tears

I feel tired
after I cry.
But it is a weariness
as after a frolic in winter snow
when my mind and body
feel at last
free.

Bravery

*A*t times I feel a need to prove myself.
I act brave
when I feel frightened.
It is sometimes helpful,
for I overcome an obstacle
and discover new found strength.
Other times it is delusion.
I mock confidence,
attempt the impossible,
ignore my feelings of fear.
These are the most risky times.
Like a child on a rooftop
balancing on the eaves,
I teeter with a smile.
I am scoffing at the truth that
I am afraid.
I am risking more than danger—
I am risking honesty.
How easily I could fall from my perch
sliding down the rooftop of false confidence,
falling in a heap of humiliation.
Courage is not foolish, dishonest bravery.
Courage is knowing my weakness
and calling on God in my fear.

Singular

I was going to make it.
I would be the one—
change this world
by age forty at least.
I would make my mark.

But the world moves on.
Forty comes
and slips away
in sighs.
I am not going to do it.
It is not done.

Am I the only one to fail?
Or is part of my search
realizing and accepting
who I am not
as well as who I am?
I am only one
still—the only one
ever to be me.
Significant mystery.

Regret

When I stop to think
of all the foolish things I've done,
I'm inclined to smile
and then to hunch my shoulders
in shame and regret.
I think of all the people
I could have hurt
or did
as I made hasty choices
or spoke carelessly
or remained silent.
I recall the selfish acts
rationalized,
"I must do this for me."
Some of them become the smile
of wisdom—
my youthful mistakes
understood from new perspective.
Others still cause my stomach
to wrench a bit
my eyes to crinkle as
I try to forget.
All those past choices
are forgiven
but memorable
and I am left,
leaning on the mercy of God.

Shielding Ourselves

*C*autiously we enter life and faith,
hiding from rain
   dreading mistakes
   terrified of poverty
and cornering ideas
so that we might pretend
to know the truth
and not have to face the questions
that plague us at night
just before sleep.
Doubting our strength,
our capacity in pain,
we arrange life
so that we have no risks
few confrontations,
superficial commitments,
and hasty, slick answers
to disturbing questions
about ourselves
or life or God.
The truth we speak we do not own.
The ones we love are already proven.
And when we die, will they say
this nice person came and went,
or this human being *lived?*

Awkward

The young man walked among the crowd,
    clumsy,
unkempt,
a shaggy beard, drooping mouth,
and unable to speak clearly.
He was different.
I watched him as he went
from one person to another
seeking conversation, friendship.
He would sit for a moment,
chew his nails,
talk earnestly,
then awkwardly move to another chair.
He came to sit beside me.
Leaning forward, he asked,
"Do you know me?"
I was nervous,
and I stabbed him with a hasty
"No."
He didn't see my afterthought,
a weak smile.
He moved away,
to search for someone who might better
overcome personal discomfort
and accept the wholeness of the young man
unqualified.

Capital Punishment

When I was small
    I watched dad kill a chicken.
Headless, it ran foolishly
until its body ceased to function.
So it is with frogs—
they jump.

Yesterday on television
six men were executed
for treason—
whatever that verdict ultimately means.
There were pictures,
close-ups
so that I might know what it is
to be shot to death.
One man was sullen,
one shouted his cause to the crowd,
some were fearful.
I was horrified.
They shot them;
bullets jarring their frames
many times—
and the camera let me watch
if I wanted to.
I closed my eyes in shock
but opened them again to find
that humans, like small animals,
do not cease to live
concisely—
they linger in moans.

Before my eyes was the vivid, violent
reality of a death of punishment.
The moans and
fear in the eyes of real people
reaffirmed my belief—
that alive,
humanity might change, hope and grow.
Dying,
they are but chickens and frogs.

Prisons

*I*t's easier to scold
  criticize
    second-guess
than it is to help
constructively.
Prisons of the state,
  full of tears.
Prisons of poverty,
    people who begin every day
    one, two, twenty
    steps behind—
    never caught up.
Prisons of sickness
    or loneliness
    or the discomfort
    or the socially inept.

I'd rather criticize
    than change—
I'd rather subtly gloat
than to reach out to help.
Then I wonder,
What if Christ is in the prison?

Unemployed

*T*he man waits in a line
   going nowhere.
He wants work—
worth,
reason to be.
He wants more than bread—
dignity.
He waits.
The man in search of life
is dying.

Urbanization

*T*he brownstone
has a yellow and a red and a blue door
to brighten the morning
where old men walk the sidewalks
alone
and the children run and wrestle
waiting on the corner for a school bus.
This is a place
where Native America has come
to hide from the reality
of broken dreams and blistered futures.
Life, here,
is rooted in the transience
of bitter winters,
steaming summers,
part-time homes,
and hopelessness.

Business As Usual

*A*cross the street
a person
jumped off the top of the building.
"Swandive," the man in the elevator quipped.
In our office, no one knew.
It's air conditioned here
with musak, whether or not you want it.
And we have original artwork
on walnut paneled walls.
If the man on the elevator
hadn't told me
we would never know that
a person
didn't choose to live anymore,
but chose to announce it to the world
right across the street
from our quiet world of business.

Vengeance

*T*oday vengeance was more than a
   television cowboy's lynching.
It was hoarded words,
ragged and barbed,
unleashed with the sharp finality
of calculated destruction.
To get even.
To feel justified!
Today vengeance was cruel and
it was me.

Belonging

She's worried about her son.
He's scared and angry
and when he doesn't know
what to do or
who to trust
he runs.
He runs away from school
or home
and they can only hope
he'll never run away
from life itself.
He's a good person
but his mother says
he's not one of the
"beautiful people"
who others easily notice
or fuss over.
Isn't he important too?
Pray for the child
who only wants to belong
and to feel capable,
a contributor to the world
and part of life
even when he isn't
one of the "beautiful people."

Prophesy

*M*y friend is going through his mid-life crisis.
He'd heard about it from all his friends
and secretly scoffed at the jargon,
the stereotypes,
the ways in which society labels people
and everybody tries their best
to fit the category made for them.
He was different.
But lately there's been a gradual change.
He rather likes sitting still
and wants to talk more with his kids
and dreams about not working
or going on a long drive by himself
and thinking.
It's a scary time
but rather interesting, too.
Mid-life.
Unfortunately, the kids are too busy to talk.
They were around five years ago
when he had meetings every night 'til eight.
Vacations then were squeezed between
the next board meeting
and the presentation to the staff
for which he'd felt peculiarly responsible.
They had to leave town and it took ten days
before he could finally wind-down.
Now kids are much more entertained by friends
and won't admit they'd even like to talk to dad.

Last week he got a nice award
for all his work with volunteers and clerks
plus his design for reassigning management.
He felt proud for a while
and brought the non-glare, gold-framed honor home.
It sat on his dresser as he combed his hair.
Then he stopped.
The hair was graying and the honor tarnished
when he recalled he couldn't "take it with him."
Mid-life crisis was more than a label
and the house he loved felt strangely empty.

HEALING AND HOPE

"And the people all tried to touch him,
because power was coming from him and healing them all."
(Luke 6:19)

Friendly Protection

*D*o not gather in all your pain
and hide it in a box,
putting it away on a shelf.
For pain will always
steal away in the middle of the night
and come to haunt you.
Rather, tell your friends
that you have pain.
And tell your pain
that you have friends!
Name the agony
and tell it how you hate it
until you are too weary to say any more.
Then set it aside on a shelf.
It may steal out some day
but it will not haunt you
because you have friends
who know and understand.

Siblings

*B*rothers, they grew up
as brothers often do,
competing.
One intimidated with his size,
another with a facile tongue.
Each succeeded in his goals
and went his way,
loyal, but hardly friends.
Then mother nearly died
and they needed each other
in a new way,
one drawing strength from the other.
Every day, between hospital calls,
they had lunch together
and talked.
A new bond was forged,
because they needed the strengths
they used to fear in each other.
Brothers, at last.

After Divorce

*H*ard to heal
and slow.
To be drawn back in memory
but battered again in pain.
To let our fingers relax,
long tensed against vulnerability,
and release clutched dreams
disappointments,
and anger.
Slowly we ease into trust,
frightened to be hurt,
knowing pain to be
more than words,
deep and real.
Pain, stay away!
We cannot hurt anymore.
This has been enough.

Then, as turning leaves
are accentuated by warm sun,
we hear ourselves sigh the longing,
the truth
that one cannot always be alone
on guard.
We are afraid,
but we begin to know
that someday we will go on.
Healing has begun.

Comfort

*H*e comes to greet us
his smiling pleasantries
muffled by his aching and tired body,
sick with cold.
Unconsciously
he reaches for his wife,
rests his hands on her shoulder and
touches her arm
as if to be warmed by her
presence.
They do not speak,
but he is made more whole,
more healthy,
comforted
by the unspoken touch of love
conveyed through his seeking hands.

Birthday Memorial

*E*ach year, on his birthday, they gather
to celebrate the life of this son
who died at twenty-five
when his life had only just begun.
It is bittersweet,
  sad
   and glad.
One might wonder why it's done.

"We choose to remember those we've loved,
to honor their part of our lives,
their contribution, their gift to us.
Better to remember the day
God gave us his life
than to concentrate on the day
he left us behind.
We do not go to the cemetery
with our tears.
We go to the fountain of Life."

Strangers

As I left the hospital
I went to my car, pensive.
Then I saw a woman,
a stranger,
walking toward her car,
tears brimming
of shaky spirit and alone.
"Are you all right?"
I asked as I moved toward her.
She was a small person,
and I, tall.
I reached out to enclose her
in my arms as she wept.
"My grandfather died," she said.
"He was very sick
but I'll miss him so much.
He was a good man."
There was little for me to reply
and in a few moments she told me
she was better now
and we parted.
I never knew her name.
Only her pain.

Kenny

*H*e was a tall, handsome boy,
  black, strong
and he came to us withdrawn,
hiding from his reality.
His father shot his mother
dead before the child's eyes,
terrorizing to one so young.
He did not speak.
He did not play.
We watched, bewildered.

One day, our teacher told us
Kenny needed friends,
understanding.
Patiently we tried—
called him over,
sat beside him,
even when his tennis shoes were smelly
(he didn't have a mother),
complimented, helped
and finally, he talked!
Children help each other heal.

We Expect Too Much

Sometimes
we expect too much from life—
unfailing health
and repeated successes,
days without quarrels,
nights without fear,
and children forever polite.
In our disappointment
we dismiss or carelessly ignore
the small but wonderful events
which offer us joy—
the kiss of a puppy,
and relief of fresh rain,
reconciliation after fighting,
autumn color every fall,
and God's promise
that despite our disappointments
we will never be alone
nor forgotten.
We are forgiven
and loved.

Overload

*I*t was Christmas.
Everything had come apart.
Grandma had cancer,
children were fighting,
and the house was full of company.
Everyone at work was overloaded
and the presents sat, unwrapped.
Every day they waited news.
Would grandma heal?
She was depressed.
Was surgery required
and was she strong enough
to make it through?
Daily he was phoning relatives
and trying to explain the illness,
while his wife battled fatigue
and overexcited children in school.
One evening it all broke.
They yelled at each other,
again and then again.
Suddenly, he sat down at the kitchen table
and wept.
He couldn't tolerate any more.
He wept
and soon she stood beside him
tears mingling with his.
In a while they took time
to be alone together.
They talked and talked,
reviewing all the pressures—

family and festival expectations.
They wept
and slept
and began again together.
Looking back, he told me
"It was in the depths
that we found hope
in each other."

Intimacy

*I*ntimate
had become a word referring to
perfume or sex,
or risqué movie scenes.
Then one day
a virtual stranger
looked me straight in the eye
and said with sincerity,
"I think I understand how you feel.
Let me tell you what happened to me."
I was surprised
and I felt shy.
It was an intimate moment.

My eyes were opened.
Intimate became, for me,
a tender, compassionate,
honest, close,
personal offering of selves.
Intimate.

Retreat

*I*t is good
in the safety of
a quiet place.
One can trust
amidst the sounds of only nature.
One can even cease to listen.
The mind and soul
can smooth the wrinkles of the
hurried life
in a quiet place.

Battle

We raged at each other,
    mother and son,
battling for pride,
    for power,
determined to win.
"You never . . .
    you always . . . !"
Declarations of blame
wounding the other,
stubbornly at bay,
until we tired
and walked away.
After an hour,
my son came to me quietly.
"I'm sorry, mom.
Can you understand how I feel?"
My eyes glistened as I nodded.
He was not too proud to bend.

Change

*A*utumn comes
and we resist, dreading change
until we relax and reassess
the values of quiet winter.
Life does not pour its sand
neatly into hourglasses,
but shifts with time and circumstance,
always forming a new design,
a new Self,
another beginning.

Flash of Light

*K*nowing dad had died
     and that she had not been there
to say good-bye,
she walked into the January morning
chilled,
and gray as its heavy skies.
From a bare branch
high above the frozen earth,
came a flash of red
and the bright whistle of a cardinal
which stopped her motion.
God had offered
a contrast of hope.
Life would go on.

Promise

*I*n late winter, it is the crocus
who helps my spirit survive.
In my miseries of self-doubt,
it's my friend.
When the airplane shakes,
I think of my destination reunion.
In the ninth month,
it's the hope of a child.
When our hands are feeble
and knees are weak,
we need promises,
hope,
a reason to wait or to try again.
The promise of God is and
was always there.
I see it in the crocus
and babies and friends—
God with us, with me.

When life is good, or life is hard, it is helpful to have Bible references on which to draw. The following abbreviated list may be useful to you.

Where to turn in times of:
Gratitude and Joy:
Psalm 8; 103; 148; Isaiah 55; Phil. 4:4-9

Believing:
Psalm 42; Isaiah 40; John 1:1-18; 3:16-17; 1 Peter 2:1-10

Loss and Mourning:
Psalm 28; John 14:1-6; 20:1-18; Rom. 8:31-39; Rev. 21:1-4

Suffering:
Psalm 34; Isaiah 42:1-4; 43:1-2; Matt. 28:1-10; John 15:12-17

Struggle:
Psalm 23; 121; Isaiah 40:1-11; Matt. 4:1-11; 5:1-12

Healing and Hope:
Matt. 11:2-5; Mark 5:21-43; Luke 5:17-26; John 11:1-27; 14:25-27